Religious Humor

409 Bits Of Humor For Preachers, Teachers, And Public Speakers

WALTER M. BUESCHER

CSS Publishing Company, Inc.
Lima, Ohio

RELIGIOUS HUMOR

Library of Congress Cataloging-in-Publication Data

Religious humor : 409 bits of humor and ecclesiastical wisdom : divided four ways, clergy, God & bible, laity, stewardship / (collected by) Walter Buescher.
   p. cm.
  includes index
  ISBN 0-07880-0707-6 (pbk.)
  1. Religious—Humor. I. Buescher, Walter M.
PN6231.R4R45   1996
818'.540208—dc20   95-25439
                                         CIP

Available in the following formats, listed by ISBN:
0-7880-0707-6 Book
0-7880-0708-4 IBM 3 1/2 computer disk
0-7880-0709-2 Macintosh computer disk

PRINTED IN U.S.A.

Dedication

My sense of humor comes from my father
Martin F. Buescher
Teacher at St. Paul's, Bremen, Indiana,
for 47 years,
also Organist, Choir Director, Sexton

Table Of Contents

Preface

Recently I read that there will be no humor in heaven. That shook me. I almost cancelled my reservation. The philosopher who came up with the observation reasoned this way: Humor is based on man's imperfections and in heaven there will be no imperfections. The assumption had a sort of $2+2=4$ validity, but I can't quite picture heaven without music, joy, and laughter.

Have you ever dissected humor to see what it has in it that makes people laugh? Much of humor is rooted in tragedy. Someone slips on a banana peel. The person with the injured tailbone doesn't think it's funny, but everybody laughs. The pastor's notes blow off the pulpit. The congregation considers the mishap to be to be hilarious. Someone gets a pie in the face at a church social. We laugh. We laugh at others' tragedies.

Much of humor is based on stupidity. For instance: "He quit racing because he kept getting lost on the track." There's much of this kind of humor in this book; this time with an ecclesiastical slant.

I'm guessing that those who have the gift of a sense of humor from above — and it is a gift — are also the people who know only too well their social shortcomings. We feel a kinship with others who, at times, also lack common sense. It's "old home week" when we're with people who are as lacking as we are. It makes us feel more human, less divine. We feel more comfortable in the role of "poor miserable sinner" than saint.

This book contains bits of religious humor that I've picked up since high school days. At one time or another, almost every story has found its way into one of my speeches, class discussions, or scripts. There were church youth leadership days and days when I taught Bible Class. There were speeches at church gatherings. The collection of humor in this book pulls no punches. Like the Bible says: there's no distinction between Jew and Greek. There is a jab at every stuffed shirt in pulpit or pew, whatever the denomination, race, occupation, or ethnic group. The humor in this book lovingly embraces all that is godly, and some things that are not quite saintly.

Don't you feel sorry for a person who can't laugh? That person must live a miserable life. You know — the kind of folks who, in their misery, enjoy very bad health, or once in a while complain of feeling better. For our personal well-being, we must laugh at ourselves at regular intervals. When we take ourselves too seriously, we are a minority of one. We must be able to laugh at ourselves, our spouses, our kids, our parents, our bosses, our preachers/rabbis/priests, our lay people, and the man-made canon law of our religious denomination.

Enjoy!

Walt Buescher

Chapter 1

Clergy

---

1. A preacher, looking for a discount, said, "I'm only a poor preacher."
   Said the clerk, "I know. I heard you."

2. Recipe for a good sermon:
   "Ah tells dem what Ah's gwine to tell dem, den Ah tells dem, and den Ah tells dem wot Ah done tole 'em."

3. A nun placed a six-pack in her grocery cart. She said it was for "her hair."
   The grocer plunked a bag of pretzels alongside the beer. "You'll need some curlers."

4. "Thank, praise, serve, and obey God." Martin Luther.

5. A bellhop said about the preachers' convention: "They come with the Ten Commandments in one hand and a ten spot in the other and don't break either one the whole time they're here."

6. A filling station attendant: "They wait until the last minute, even though the trip was planned a year ago."
   A preacher: "Works the same in my business, too."

7. At St. Mary's the priest won a set of his/her towels at a raffle.
   Someone advised him, "Better keep them. With things going the way they are, you may need them some day."

8. Despite a severely limited budget, the wife of a new ordinand bought herself a pretty dress for Easter.

Her husband rebuked her: "When you were tempted to buy it, you should have said, 'Get thee behind me, Satan.' "

"That's what I did say," the minister's wife replied, "and Satan whispered, 'It looks very nice from the back.' "

9. Two chaplains were lost on the battlefront. Then they heard someone say, "Who in the hell led the ace?"

They looked at each other and smiled. One said, "Thank God, we're among Christians again."

10. Dad criticized the sermon. Mother thought the organist did a lousy job. Sister didn't like the choir's singing.

Junior: "All in all, I thought it was a good show for a buck."

11. The priest issued some orders about birth control.

Lady with six kids: "If you donna playa da game, you donna maka da rules."

12. "Does your dad prepare a new sermon for every Sunday?"
"Naw, he just yells in different places."

13. Pastor at baptism: "And what is the baby's name, please?"
"Robert William Montgomery Morgan Maxwell III."
"More water, please."

14. A preacher bought a used car and didn't have the vocabulary to run it.

15. It's a wise man who knows that the church is bigger than the preacher or any of the laity.

16. A missionary carried a gun and a Bible. The gun was for tigers who either couldn't read or weren't Presbyterian.

17. Sister Teresa entered a convent at Trans, France, and became a Trans-sister.

18. Everybody liked the new preacher's first sermon. He kept repeating it Sunday after Sunday.
    "Parson, aren't we ever going to get a new sermon?"
    "When I get action on the old one."

19. At a civic banquet, they were honoring Ace Mfg. Company's 75 years in business.
    "Is there a representative of a business older than that in the room?"
    Pastor: "I have that honor, sir."

20. The new church had automated pews. When the people sat in the back, the preacher pushed a button and a conveyor belt moved them up front. He was overjoyed until his sermon went a little overtime and the pulpit lowered into the basement automatically.

21. At a revival meeting, Joe was confessing his sins. He went on for a long time.
    Preacher: "Hold it, Joe. Are you confessin' or braggin'?"

22. "That's a mighty fine crop you and the Lord have there."
    "Thank you, Reverend, but you should have seen it when the Good Lord was farmin' this place all by himself."

23. A preacher drove like a madman. His passenger said, "You better be more careful, Reverend."

Pastor: "The Lord's watching over me."

Passenger: "I got news for you. The Lord got out at that last stop light."

24. When the Ark sprung a leak, Noah had a dog hold his nose over the leak. There was too much water for the dog, so Noah's wife stood over the hole. She couldn't contain the water either, so Noah sat on the hole.

To this day, a dog's nose is always cold. Women always have cold feet and men stand with their back to the stove or fireplace.

25. The preacher preached on sin. First he preached against gin and everybody said, "amen." Then he worked on crap shooting and everybody said "amen." Then he began to berate wild women. A woman in the congregation said, "Preacher, you has quit preachin' and has started in to meddlin'."

26. There was a baptizing at the river. "I'm going to baptize you in this stream and take every bit of sin away that you got."

"In that li'l old shallow crick?"

27. A pastor was known for his counseling skills. He had so many people come that he decided to do group counseling. He scheduled a session for ten people at a time, but when the time came, he was delayed and came late. When he got there, only one person was present.

"We got to comparing notes and decided that our troubles were insignificant to the troubles that others had, so the other nine left. They told me to thank you."

28. Pastor's wife: "My dear, haven't you forgot to ask the blessing?"

Pastor: "If you can see anything on this table that hasn't been blessed at least three times, point it out to me."

29. When the pastor came to visit, only Junior was at home. "Where's your dad?"

Junior: "He's at the golf club."

Pastor: "He's at the golf club on a Sunday?"

Junior: "Oh, he ain't playin' golf. He just went over for a few drinks and a few hands of stud poker."

30. The preacher finished a long-distance prayer. Junior asked his mother, "What did he say?"

Mother: "He said a prayer for the people in the service."

Junior: "The 8:30 or 10:30 service?"

31. A lot of the hierarchy thought that when the new Pope was named, it would be Cardinal Sicola. He wasn't chosen.

"Why do you suppose they passed you up?"

"I'm guessing that they didn't want someone named Pope Sicola."

32. A priest and preacher got a free drink at the airport bar by pretending that they had already paid at the crowded bar. A rabbi tried the same trick, but then the plane was called. Everybody rushed to the gate and there were only a few left in the bar. The bartender told the rabbi how he had almost double-charged a preacher and a priest.

The rabbi replied, "Don't tell me your troubles. Give me my change and let me get out of here."

33. A parishioner offered the preacher a quarter of his home-made brandy provided the pastor acknowledged the gift in the church bulletin. The pastor accepted. He wrote:

"My hearty thanks to Brother Beavers for his gift of fruit, and the spirit in which it was given."

34. The pulpit-thumping preacher was wound up on sin. He was really letting his parishioners smell the flesh burning and hear the cries of agony.

Then a good-looking, shapely young woman in a miniskirt came down the aisle and sat in the front row, crossing her legs. The preacher leaned over to the deacon and whispered, "Isn't that Fanny Green?"

"No, that's only the light coming through the stained glass window."

35. Twice the priest made the sign of the cross and twice the horse won. When a layman tried it, his horse died on the track. He complained to the priest.

"You must be Protestant," said the priest. "You don't know the difference between a blessing and the last rites."

36. The service started late. The organist slowly accompanied the congregation through all seventeen verses of the hymn. Brother Smith had a nonstop prayer. To get back on schedule, the preacher preached:

"Last night you raised it. Today you look like it. And soon you'll be there. Amen."

37. The preacher told his flock, "We're told today to accept alternate lifestyles. But the Bible says it was Adam and Eve, not Adam and Steve."

38. The priest kept chanting, "And the angel lit the candles." Finally a wee small voice of an altar boy came from off-stage. He chanted, "The cat wet the matches."

39. Father O'Brien said he was a compulsive gambler.
Rabbi Goldstein said he was compulsive with women.
Rector Wellington said he was a compulsive drinker.
The Baptist preacher said, "Excuse me, I have to leave."
"Why?"
"Because I'm a compulsive gossip."

40. Rev. E. L. Tweedle turned down the offer of an honorary doctorate. "I'll be darned if I want to be known as 'Tweedle D.D.' "

41. When two nuns stood in the cold in front of the Unemployment Office waiting for a bus, one of the workers inside invited them to come in out of the cold.
Two men came to the office. When one saw the nuns, he told his buddy, "If the Pope is laying them off, there'll be no job for me."

42. A Norwegian bishop on his visit to a parish commented that there was an unreasonable amount of illegitimacy in the parish.
Pastor: "My Lord Bishop, what would you consider to be a reasonable amount of illegitimacy?"

43. An eighty-year-old retired minister stared at a beautiful young girl who passed by. "I never cease to enjoy the works of God's creation."

44. The preachers' bowling team was known as the Holy Rollers.

A bystander commented, "I've never seen so many preachers in the gutter before."

45. "You look anemic."

"No, I'm Methodist."

46. Preacher Smith chopped away at his ball in the sand trap. Finally it flew out ... into the trap on the other side of the green.

"Will some layman please utter some appropriate words?"

47. At St. Boniface, there was a talent show for the high school band. The second act was terrific. Three nuns in the front row of the balcony got up and cheered and cheered and cheered. One got so carried away that she slipped and fell overboard. Luckily she grabbed a chandelier on the way down. She swung over the crowd.

The monsignor noticed this and ran to the mike: "Anyone who looks up will be struck blind."

"Pat, what are you gonna do?"

"I think I'll risk one eye."

48. A nun came screaming out of the doctor's office.

"What happened?"

"I told her she was pregnant."

"She isn't, is she?"

"No, but it cured her hiccups."

49. A pastor's wife wrote a book titled, "How Green Was My Pastor."

50. The Benedictine monks at Maria Lach have been singing the same *Te Deum* as they walk single-file to vespers, since the year 1182 when the monastery was founded. They started chanting about the glory of God before Abelard preached his heresies in Paris, before Luther nailed his 95 theses, before Columbus discovered America, before Hitler and Stalin tried to destroy the world and destroyed themselves instead.

51. In Africa, a lion came toward the missionary. The pastor prayed fervently. The lion lay down and bowed his head. ✓
The missionary said, "Thank you, dear Lord."
The lion said, "Bless this meal of which I am about to partake."

52. The Pope named Arnold Palmer a monsignor so he could play for the Catholics in the ecumenical council's golf tournament. He came in second, right behind Rabbi Snead. ✓

53. A Methodist minister was asked to bury a Baptist neighbor. He asked the bishop about it and the bishop replied:
"By all means, bury all of the Baptists you can."

54. The preacher preached for 46 minutes. He had gotten his wife's teeth by mistake and couldn't stop.

55. "Reverend, something has to be done about my Willie. He no longer comes home at night to me and our eight kids. Instead, he's all over town drinking, gambling, and running with wild women."
"You have my deepest sympathy, Mary. Your husband is a miserable sinner."
"Sinner, yes; but miserable, no. He's having the time of his life."

56. Martin Luther wrote a book titled, "I Was a Teenage Roman Catholic."

57. Two preachers differed on doctrine.
"That's okay. We're both doing the Lord's work; you in your way and I in the Lord's way."

58. The holy water froze and they had popesicles.

59. A priest gave a young girl a ride. She was obviously drunk.
She kept saying, "You're passionate."
He didn't pick up on the cue, but kept asking where she lived.
"I've been tryin' to tell you — you're passin' it."

60. A man of the cloth came to town, got in a cab and asked to be taken to a haberdashery.
The cab driver didn't know where to go but was afraid to say so. However, finally he asked, "Is that liquor or women?"

61. A priest called his bishop. "There's a parade coming toward the church. There's a man out in front who is in a white robe and he has a long beard. What should I do?"
"Be nice to him. It may be the boss."

62. A priest said that hearing the confessions of nuns was like being stoned with popcorn.

63. A nun had a few too many. She got up and shaped her hand so that it looked like a gun. She said, "Bang, bang, bang."

Her confessor told her that tomorrow night, when sober, she should do the same thing. She did and this time she said, "Click, click, click." She wasn't loaded that evening.

64. A Lutheran preacher wore a clerical collar in an Irish neighborhood. Kids saw him coming down the street.

"That's the Lutheran Father at St. Paul's."

"He's no father — he's got three kids."

65. A Catholic bishop gave this advice:

"Build a bar in your own house. Buy a quart of whiskey. Have your wife sell it to you at $3 per drink — 16 drinks to the quart. By the time you consume the first quart, your wife will have $38 net profit. Let's say you live ten years and then you die of the DTs. Your wife will have plenty of money with which to bury you. She can then marry a decent man and forget about the misery you brought her."

66. A preacher timed his sermon with a cough drop. One Sunday he went on endlessly. He had put a button in his mouth.

67. "Let us pray this morning for those of our parishioners who are on beds of sickness and davenports of wellness."

68. Mike said he didn't go into the priesthood because of the money. He told the people of his parish, "There's a heck of a good retirement plan."

69. Rev. Morrison rang the bell but nobody answered the door, so he left a note: "Rev. 3:20." Revelation 3:20 reads, "Behold I stand at the door and knock. If any man hear my voice, and open the door, I will come in to him."
The next Sunday the lady of the house gave the preacher a card that said: "Gen. 3:10." This passage reads, "I heard thy voice in the garden, and I was afraid because I was naked, so I hid myself."

70. A Kentucky preacher went to a church banquet in Indiana. When somebody asked him if he wanted some corn, he passed his glass.

71. A fashionable preacher prayed about the nation's great men. "Thank you, dear Lord, for men like Washington, Jefferson, Lincoln, and Roosevelt. That's Teddy, not Franklin, Lord."

72. Our preacher had an accident. He was trying on shoes when the wedding car drove away.

73. "Lord, fill my mouth with worthwhile stuff and nudge me when I've said enough."

74. A hill preacher told how the Lord took a handful of sand and made a man and hung him on the barbed wire fence to dry. "Then he took a handful of dust and made a woman the same way."
"Preacher, where did that barbed wire fence come from?"
"It's questions like that that is ruinin' religion."

20

75. Bishop O'Malley was MC at a banquet. He announced: "We'll wait with the entertainment until the waitresses have taken everything off."

76. A cannibal ate three missionaries and then had an ecumenical movement.

77. The new preacher in Harlem was always mistaken for Louis Armstrong. He always corrected the mistake. When he was introduced to a beautiful young lady, she said, "Why, you're Louis Armstrong!"
And he said, "Hello, Dolly."

78. When a preacher says "finally" in his sermon, he doesn't necessarily mean "immediately."

79. A priest was eyeing a good-looking member of the parish.
"Father, you surprise me."
"Just because I'm on a diet doesn't mean I can't look at the menu."

80. When the preacher came for Sunday dinner he cleaned the serving plate of two fried chickens. Walking around the farm after dinner, the pastor saw a rooster and remarked that the rooster looked very proud.
His host exclaimed, "He should be. He now has two children in the holy ministry."

81. A priest in sports clothes was conned into a big bet at the golf course. The priest lost $50. When his opponent found out that he had been playing with a priest, he offered to give the money back.
Priest: "Never mind. Just send your mother and father around sometime and I'll marry them."

82. At the ecumenical affair, the Baptist preacher won the opening door prize — a bottle of Jack Daniels. The closing door prize was won by the local rabbi — a canned ham. Chairman: "Let the minutes show that Brother Smith won the closing door prize and Rabbi Rabbinovitz the opening door prize."

83. "I prayed for you last night, Widow Brown." "Why didn't you call? I would have been right over."

84. A visiting clergyman came to a city to deliver two speeches. After the first speech in the morning, he told the reporter for an afternoon newspaper, "In your article, don't mention the two stories I told. I want to use them again this evening."

The newspaper report of the morning meeting read: "Reverend Glickman told two stories that cannot be published."

85. A preacher picked up the phone. He recognized the voice as that belonging to one of his parishioners. It was obviously a wrong number because the request was, "Bring two quarts of Scotch to the poker game tonight, Mulligan."

"Mrs. Beckwith, this is not Mr. Mulligan. It is your pastor."

"What are you doing in Mulligan's Tap, Reverend?"

86. You'll recall that Pope John XXIII brought congregational singing to the mass. One priest had his parish people practice hymn singing. When they concluded he paid his flock the ultimate compliment, "You know, you're singing as good as Lutherans do."

87. Preachers do not talk in their sleep — they talk in their parishioners' sleep.

88. A nun in a contemplative order was allowed to speak one sentence every ten years. Her first utterance was: "I don't like the food." Ten years later she said, "I don't like the beds." Thirty years went by and she said, "I don't like either the food or beds and I sure would like to get out of here."

Mother Superior: "Then why don't you go. Ever since you've been here, it has been nothing but gripe, gripe, gripe."

89. A Boston pastor returned a purse to a woman who had left it in the pew. "Mrs. Flint, I must remind you that a purse left in such a manner might be considered, for some individuals, to be an answer to prayer."

90. Preaching in older days had occupational hazards:

Matthew was slain by a sword in Ethiopia.

Mark was dragged through the streets of Alexandria and died.

Luke was hanged in Greece.

John was dumped into a cauldron of boiling oil but escaped.

James the Great was beheaded in Jerusalem.

James the Lesser was thrown from the pinnacle of the temple.

Philip was hanged in Heropolis.

Bartholomew was flogged to death.

Andrew was crucified.

Thomas was lanced to death in the East Indies.

Jude was shot with arrows and died.

Matthias was stoned and then beheaded.

Barnabas was stoned to death.

Peter was crucified head down.

Paul was beheaded.

91. A visiting pastor arrived at the church with his son. So that his son could see his good deed, he placed $2 in the "poor box." After the service, the deacons said they were sorry but had no money with which to pay the visiting clergyman. They said the crops had done poorly. What crops the grasshoppers missed were knocked down by hail. Then one of the deacons remembered the "poor box." He brought the $2 and paid the pastor. "It's not much, Reverend, but it's better than nothing."

On the way home, the pastor told his son, "Let that be a lesson to you — the more you give to the Lord the more you get back. If I had put $5 in that 'poor box,' I would have been paid $5 for the sermon."

92. A hill preacher rode a beautiful horse.

"Reverend, why does your horse look so good and you look so shabby?"

"I take care of the horse. The congregation takes care of me."

93. Some louse threw a rock through the church's stained-glass window. The trustees temporarily placed a piece of cardboard in the window to replace the glass.

The next Sunday, the preacher preached, "I often feel like that piece of cardboard — I'm surrounded by so much beauty."

On the way out of church, one of the parishioners consoled the pastor, "You'll always be a real pane to me."

94. At a Southern church social, the group sat in a circle and each was supposed to tell what he/she thought was the best thing in life.

One said, "Chicken." One said, "Watermelon." A sister said, "Parson, you better stop this right here before somebody tells the truth."

24

95. A preacher threw up his money. What landed in a circle on the floor went to the Lord. The rest he kept.

A priest threw up his money. What landed on the right side of a line, he gave to the church. The money landing on the left side of the line went into his pocket.

A rabbi threw up his money. He figured if the Lord wanted some of it, he would help himself.

96. Did you ever see a U-Haul trailer behind a hearse?

97. The Mother Superior ordered oil for the convent before winter set in.

"What's the price this year?"

The oil man said, "Are you sitting down?"

"No, I'm kneeling."

98. "The first two days of the revival I preach them into hell. The last three days I preach them into heaven."

99. They went to Yankee Stadium to see the Pope. A drunk in back yelled, "Batter up." I yelled back, "This is not a ball game. The Pope is coming out soon." Then the drunk yelled, "Bingo."

100. A literal preacher said, "I'm going to open my Bible in three places and do what the Bible tells me to do."

The first time he opened the Book to "And Judas went out and hanged himself."

The second reading was, "What I do, do thou likewise."

The third: "What thou doest, do so quickly."

101. Two nuns returned from Ireland. The Customs Agent, going through their belongings, came upon a half-filled bottle. The nuns said it was holy water. The Customs Agent took a sniff. "Smells like Irish whiskey to me."

"Praise the Lord, another miracle of Cana."

102. A country preacher preached on the sinfulness of dancing. He painted vivid word pictures of the sensual desires that dancing unleashed. He spoke of vertical expression of horizontal desire.

Commenting on the sermon at Sunday lunch, one member of the family said, "I don't know if you kids dance or not, but one thing for sure, I know our preacher shouldn't dance."

103. "After living forty-odd years among good people, I can understand why Christ chose to spend most of his time among sinners."

104. A preacher was speaking about the prophets. "Hezekiah — where will we place him?"

A parishioner replied, "He can have my seat. I'm going home."

105. Walking along the Embarcadero in San Francisco, a pastor walked with his two young nieces. They saw a fisherman mending his nets. The preacher told the man he was a fisherman, too — "I fish for men."

"You're sure using good bait, Reverend."

106. After having been fed jackrabbit in every form in Texas, a preacher, at his bishop's house, was served rabbit in a silver chafing dish. He said:

"Oh Lord, I've had them young and I've had them old.

I've had them hot and I've had them cold.

I've had them tender and I've had them tough.

But oh, my God, I've had enough. Good-bye."

107. "That was a damn good sermon, Reverend."

"Thanks, but don't you think the compliment was a bit strong?"

"I put a $100 bill in the collection plate."

"The hell you did."

108. As he boarded the commuter, the forgetful bishop couldn't find his train ticket. The conductor said, "Oh, that's all right. I know who you are and that you've paid."

"Yes, but I need the ticket to know where to get off."

109. The preacher was explaining the difference between faith and knowledge.

"Now take the Simpson family, there. She *knows* that the three children sitting with them are hers. He *believes* that the kids are his. That's faith."

110. The church bulletin board read: "One faith. One church. One hour."

111. A pastor called the Health Department to remove a dead mule from the street in front of his house.

"I thought that preachers took care of the dead."

"We do, but we notify the next of kin first."

112. Sign on Catholic drive-in confessional:

"Toot and tell or go to hell."

113. The Bible class teacher told of the Old Testament king who had 1,000 wives and 1,000 concubines. "He fed them all ambrosia."

"Who cares what they ate? Tell us what *he* ate."

114. The wheel came off of Jimmie's bicycle. He said, "I'll be damned."

Pastor: "Instead, why don't you say, 'Praise the Lord.' "

Then both wheels came off and the kid said, "Praise the Lord." Both wheels jumped back on again.

Pastor: "Well, I'll be damned."

115. Earmarks of a good pastor: (1) He can comfort the distressed, and (2) he can distress the comfortable.

116. Two nuns ran out of fuel near the Irish border. They walked to a nearby farmhouse. The farmer said, "I have some bloody petrol, but I have nothing to put it in, don't y'know." He rooted around in the junk behind the barn and came up with an old chamber pot that had been thrown out years before. He filled the old sanitation vessel with fuel and gave it to the nuns.

They thanked the farmer profusely, then walked back to the motorcar and started to pour the petrol into the tank.

An Anglican stopped and said, "I'm not Catholic, Sisters, but I certainly admire your faith, that I do."

117. A preacher moaned that he had deacons who wouldn't deke — trustees he couldn't trust — and stewards who got stewed.

118. Doctor's kid: "All my dad has to do to make money is go to the hospital and operate on somebody and he gets $3,000."

Lawyer's kid: "All my dad has to do is to go to a courtroom and talk for a day and he makes $7,000."

Minister's kid: "When my dad talks for a half hour in church, it takes four men to bring the money to him."

28

119. Groom: "Pastor, how much do I owe you?"
Pastor: "Take a look at your bride and tell me what she is worth to you."
He got $10. The preacher looked at the girl and gave the man $5 change.

120. The pastor scheduled a wedding right after the Sunday morning worship service. ✓
"Will the persons who wish to be married step forward?"
One man and thirteen women came forward.

121. An abandoned car with a case of whiskey on the back seat was found in front of the church. The evening paper reported: "The Rev. Simpson is working on that case."

122. A society lady invited the bishop to share her box at the opera. Looking through opera glasses, the bishop observed ↙ other society ladies with low-cut gowns being ushered to their seats.
"Honestly, Bishop, have you ever seen anything like this in all your life?"
The good bishop replied, "Not since I was weaned."

123. Baptist preacher during a drought: "Lord, we're not asking for a frog-strangling gully-washer. All we ask you for is a three-day tizzy-tazzy."

124. Baptist preacher: "If someone gave me a truckload of whiskey, I would drive it into the river. Now let us turn to hymn #167 and sing, 'Let Us Gather By The River.' "

125. When the late Dr. O. P. Kretzman, president of Valparaiso University, addressed the Alumni Association, he said: "Before we went in to see the Pope, we were given instructions about what to wear and what to say. Women were told that they should wear black; dresses up to the neck, down to the elbows and ankles. A disrespectful Irishman in the crowd asked, 'Wouldn't it be easier to blindfold the Holy Father?' "

126. Since the pulpit was tall and the preacher was short, he stood on a box. However, one Sunday someone filched the box. He stood in the pulpit with his horn-rims barely topping the edge of the pulpit.

"This morning I'm going to preach on the subject, 'Fear not, it is I.' "

127. Before the days of turn signals ...

A cop stopped a driver because he didn't signal a turn with his arm. The driver turned out to be his pastor. "Reverend, this is the first time I've seen you that you didn't have your hand out."

128. This preacher had one foot in heaven and the other in his mouth.

129. A fashionable preacher in a fashionable church in a fashionable neighborhood sermonized fashionably, "Verily I say unto you, repent of your sins, more or less, and ask for forgiveness, in a measure, or you'll be damned, to a certain extent."

130. "How come you always fall asleep when I preach?"

"Would I fall asleep if I didn't trust you completely?"

131. "I didn't say that the preacher was a member of KKK. I said he was a wizard under the sheets."

132. The lady's parrot always said, in front of company, "Look at me, I'm a swinger." The lady's pastor suggested that he had a parrot that might be able to teach her parrot better manners. The birds were placed in a cage together. Now the lady's parrot said, "Drop your beads, Charley — my prayers are answered."

133. The preacher said it wasn't the B&O coming past the church during the service that bothered him so much as the Nickel Plate that came up to him after the sermon.

134. An Irish cop stopped a Lutheran pastor and his wife after the clergyman ran a red light. When he saw the clerical collar, the officer warned the "Father" of the roadblock ahead.
Pastor's wife: "Do you know what he thought you were?"
Pastor: "Yes, I know, but I wonder who he thought you were."

135. Col. Sanders offered the Pope a million dollars if he would change it to "Give us this day our daily chicken." The Pope said he wouldn't do it because if he did, he would lose the Wonder Bread account.

136. The Pope ordered pizza from Tony's Pizza Piazza, but Tony ran into a traffic jam on the way to the Vatican. His friend Luigi who had a pizza place close to the papal chambers helped him out. When the two met, Tony suggested that he should get half of what the Pope paid for the pizza.
Luigi said, "Okay," and he made half of a sign of the cross.

137. The Polish Pope said he was thrilled to be elected Pope, but he told his mother over the phone, "I'll be moving into an Italian neighborhood."

138. A preacher asked a boy how to get to the post office. When the boy told him, he invited the boy to come to church that night. "I'll tell you how to get to heaven."
"Tell me how to get to heaven? You don't even know the way to the post office."

139. Len lay dying.
Priest: "Have you made peace with your God?"
"Yes."
"Have you denounced the Devil?"
"The shape I'm in, Father, I don't dare antagonize anyone."

140. A traveling preacher stopped to talk to a farmer.
"It's good to see you laboring in the Lord's vineyard."
"These is soybeans, not grapes."
"Are you a Christian?"
"No, I'm Johanssen. Jim Christian lives up the road a piece."
"Are you lost?"
"No, I've lived here all my life."
"Are you prepared for the resurrection?"
"When is it?"
"Could be anytime — yesterday, today, tomorrow."
"Don't tell the missus. She'll want to go all three days."

141. Dwight Moody found a slip of paper lying on the pulpit with the word "fool" on it.
He told his congregation, "I've received anonymous letters where the author didn't sign his name, but this is the first time I've seen the writer sign his name but forget to include the letter."

142. Moses stood at the formidable Red Sea. He asked his engineer, "Can you part the waters?" He said, "No ... too much hydraulic pressure."

Moses then asked the medical officer, who replied, "Who knows what pestilence lurks at the bottom of those waters? I'd like a second medical opinion."

Moses asked his military aide. The aide came up with a lot of logistics of cots, rations, timing, budgets, boats, pontoons, and so forth. Then Moses asked his Public Relations man, "Do you think I can part those waters?"

The PR man replied, "It's a long shot, Moses, but if you get it done I'll get you five pages in the New Testament."

143. There was an untoward bit of un-Christian dissent at this rural church. To put it mildly, the parishioners didn't like their preacher. His year's contract was up. After the Wednesday night prayer meeting, the congregation assembled to discuss the matter. The preacher said, "All of you who want me to stay another year, say 'aye.' "

No one said a word.

The pastor broke the silence with, "Silence gives consent. I'm your preacher for another year. Thank you, Brethren and Sistern."

144. The Standard Oil people were meeting in the Mountain Room of the Sheraton, and Baptist pastors had an annual meeting in the Riverside Room of the same hotel. Since watermelons were in season, the chef thought it was a good idea to serve watermelon slices to both groups. The round red of a watermelon slice seemed to be so appropriate, since Standard Oil signs are often round and red. Appropriately, the chef added a little brandy to the Standard Oil slices.

Inappropriately, the Standard Oil slices were taken to the Riverside Room instead of to the Mountain Room. The mix-up was discovered too late. The chef held his head in horror. He asked, "What did the Baptist ministers say?"

A waiter replied, "They didn't say anything as far as I heard, but I saw some of the preachers putting the seeds in their pocket."

145. After the congregation sang, "Like a mighty army moves the church of God," the pastor drew a comparison between wartime armies and the armies made up of "Onward Christian Soldier" types.

"Can you picture a soldier saying, 'Captain, I was out late last night, so I couldn't come to the parade grounds this morning. However, I was with you in spirit'?"

"Do you think a soldier could get by with, 'Sorry, but I have a golf date this morning' or 'I've got guests, so don't expect me on the drill field today'?"

146. An elder told the young cleric, "Pastor, why don't you pep up your sermons a little bit? Why not use gestures? It may seem awkward at first, but just make a few simple moves. For instance, move one arm up and down."

The young pastor decided to try gestures the next Sunday. He came upon the passage, "When the roll is called up yonder, I'll be there." The message was clear, but the gestures were a disaster. He held his arm and hand high when he said, "When the roll is called up yonder." That was right, but he was wrong when he pointed down toward hell and then said, "I'll be there."

✓ 147. Parishioners didn't like the fact that the new pastor read his sermons, but they were good sermons so they were tolerated. They were good sermons because the preacher had a gifted friend who wrote good sermons. The pastor never acknowledged his friend's authorship.

One Sunday, the author got even. When the pastor came to page five, he found these words: "Improvise, Buster; improvise."

148. After seven years in the mission fields of East Africa, a Methodist missionary returned to the United States. The missionary didn't want his family to be conspicuous so they laid over in London to buy different clothes.

When the family landed at Kennedy in New York and were met by the press and a delegation of church dignitaries, the clothes were inconspicuous. The fact that the missionary's children carried their baggage on their heads, however, made for good front page pictures on the next morning's editions.

149. A young preacher wanted to make an impression on his congregation. When speaking of Christ's second coming, the young cleric pounded the pulpit and shouted, "I'm coming!" When he hit the pulpit lectern a third time, the lectern split and splinters fell down on the worshippers below.

The pastor apologized profusely to a woman below who had gotten most of the splintered wood. She said, "Think nothing of it, Pastor. You warned me twice that you were coming. I should have gotten out of the way."

150. The famous Dr. Joseph Parker of the City Temple, London, found that not all of his sermons measured up to the standards he had set for himself. After one such only-fair sermon, a young seminary student thanked him. "Doctor, I want to thank you for that sermon."

"Deceiver," thundered the great Dr. Parker.

"No, Doctor, I mean it. If the great Dr. Parker can come up with a sermon like that, there's hope for me."

Parker smiled. He answered, "Now, that's better. Wasn't it awful?"

151. Not even pastors can find the joy of the Resurrection in themselves seven days a week, 24 hours a day. Martin Luther was no exception. On one of his grumpy days, his wife Katie wore black. He asked her why.

"God is dead!"

Luther replied, "No, God is NOT dead. He's very much alive."

Then Katie came back with this squelcher: "They why don't you act like it, Martin?"

152. Upbeat preacher: "I'm proud to say that this church does not dabble in politics."

Heckler: "And religion either."

153. "I don't believe in the Bible because I don't know who the author was."

Pastor: "You don't know who the author of the multiplication tables was either. Do you believe in them?"

154. After a small town couple visited a fashionable downtown church in the city, they came home and commented, "That preacher raked with the teeth up."

155. Pastor: "Why do you hold your ball games on Sunday?"

Baseball player: "People have the day off. We get more of a crowd on Sunday. You work on Sunday, Preacher Smith?"

Pastor: "Yes, but I'm in the right field."

Player: "So am I. Isn't the sun terrible?"

156. Her pastor's sermon included these sentences, "The Lord is wise. He makes roses to bloom in the sun and fuchsia in the shade."

When the service concluded and the pastor was shaking hands with the departing parishioners, Mrs. Stillwell thanked the pastor. "Thank you, Pastor. You really helped me today." "I'm glad to hear that. In what did I help you, Mrs. Stillwell?"

"I've always wondered why I couldn't get my fuchsia to bloom."

157. Patrick Hooley operated a small store in South Minneapolis, which is heavily populated with Norwegian Lutherans. His friends coaxed him to run for alderman. "Shure, and you've got to be joshing. An Irish Catholic amongst these Norwegian Lutherans?" was Pat's usual reply. His friends persisted. He ran and was elected, not once, but three times. Then his friends suggested he run for mayor. Again, Pat demurred, claiming that he wouldn't stand a chance of being elected. Again, his friends kept coaxing. Again, he ran. Again, he was elected. Patrick Hooley was now Mayor of South Minneapolis, Minnesota!

Pastor Olaf Iverson of Lutefisk Lutheran Church invited Pat to speak during the intermission of the choir concert. Pastor Iverson's introduction of Mayor Pat at the concert was heavily laden with superlatives.

Pat was equal to the occasion. With a twinkle of multi-religiosity in his eye, Pat said, "Ladies and gentlemen, only in America! Only in America could this happen. An Irish Catholic shopkeeper. First you fine Norwegian Lutherans elected me alderman. I was flattered. Then you elected me mayor. I was humbled. Shure, and I thank Pastor Iverson for all his kind words; however in one thing, I think you've carried the approbation a bit too far, eh? Before you introduced me, Pastor Iverson, you had the choir sing, 'Hooley, Hooley, Hooley, Lord God Almighty!' "

Chapter 2

God, Bible, And Eternity

158. Saint Peter showed the new arrival around. In one room the people were dancing, drinking and carousing. "They're Baptists," Peter said. "They never had a chance to do this on earth."

In the next room the people were asleep. "These are Catholics. They did their carousing on earth and are tired."

In the next room, Peter said, "Sssh, please be quiet. These are Lutherans and they think they're the only ones up here."

159. A cab driver was given priority at the Pearly Gates. Saint Peter explained, "He scared the hell out of more people on earth than you preachers did."

160. Saint Peter kicked one couple out. "They're materialistic; her name is Penny."

He kicked another couple out. "They're alcoholics; her name is Sherry."

"Come on, Fanny, let's go. We'll never get in."

161. In heaven, when you sin, your clock jumps forward an hour.

"Where's Bill's clock?"

"Oh, we're using it in the back room as an electric fan."

162. Saint Peter gave me chalk and told me to climb the Golden Stairs, writing a sin I had committed on each step. At the 998th step, I met Joe ... coming down for more chalk.

39

163. Sign in front of church: "This is a ch--ch. What's missing?"

164. Fire trucks have four wheels and eight men. Four plus eight is twelve. There are twelve inches in a foot and a foot is a ruler. Queen Elizabeth is a ruler and also an ocean liner. The sea has fish and fish have fins. The Finns fought the Russians and the Russians are reds. Fire trucks are always rushin', so that's why fire trucks are red.

If you think this is farfetched, you should hear some excuses that people give for not attending church.

165. It's fine to pray for a good corn crop. However, if all you do is pray and you don't take the planter out of the shed, you have the wrong idea about the efficacy of prayer.

166. God takes your sins and drops them into the sea, then puts up a NO FISHING sign. They're past. They're forgotten. If you keep them alive, it's you. It's not God.

167. Bob and Judy wanted to start a new church denomination. Saint Robert didn't sound right and Judyism was already taken.

168. The Bible mentions laxatives. It says, "Behold Moses took the two tablets and went into the wilderness."

169. A little boy asked, "Why do church steeples all have plus signs on them?"

That's interesting. Christianity is certainly a plus.

170. God is like ...
   Bayer aspirin ... he works wonders.
   Ford ... he has a better idea.
   Dial ... he provides round-the-clock protection.
   Coca-Cola ... he's the real thing.
   Scope ... he makes you feel fresh.
   GE light bulbs ... he lights our path.
   Hallmark ... he cared enough to send the very best.

171. A Lutheran ...
   cast the deciding vote for the Declaration of Independence.
   rang the Liberty Bell and cracked it.
   pastor led the most famous regiment in the Revolutionary War.
   church was the site of Washington's funeral.
   Frenchman by the name of Fred Bartholdi made the Statue of Liberty.
   was the first president of the Continental Congress.
   was the first governor of Georgia.
   group came here seven years before the Puritans.

172. Religion is endorsed by so many and practiced by so few.

173. A lie is an abomination unto the Lord and a very present help in trouble.

174. To cut down on the no-shows, a Baptist church in Carlisle, Pennsylvania, offered ...

cots for those who like to sleep.

hard hats for those who say "the roof would fall in if I went to church."

blankets for those who are always cold in church.

fans for those who are always too warm.

sand for those who prefer the beach.

eyedrops for those who stayed awake all night.

cotton for the ears of those who find the organ too loud.

scorecards for those who feel that the church is full of hypocrites.

television sets for couch potatoes.

poinsettias and Easter lilies for those who only get to church on Christmas and Easter.

guides for those who prefer to worship God in nature.

175. Church bulletin board:
"If you're tired of sin, come right in."
Someone added in lipstick: "If not, call 782-5741."

176. Wherever you find four Lutherans, you'll find a fifth.

177. Democracy is a rule by the majority. But the minority can be right. Witness Jesus Christ and his handful of disciples.

178. Prayer of Saint Francis ...

Lord, make me an instrument of your peace.
Where there is hatred, let me sow love.
Where there is injury, pardon.
Where there is discord, union.
Where there is doubt, faith.
Where there is despair, hope.
Where there is darkness, light.
Where there is sadness, joy.
Grant that we may not so much seek to be consoled as to console; to be understood as to understand; to be loved as to love.
For it is in giving that we receive, it is in pardoning that we are pardoned; and it is in dying that we are born to eternal life.

179. A black man wanted to join a white church. The pastor suggested that he pray about it. The cleric later asked what the Lord said. ✓

The black man replied, "He said, 'Never mind. I've been tryin' to get into that church, too, for ten years, and I've given up.' "

180. The Puritans came to this country to worship in their own way and to force others to worship that way, too.

181. North America seems to have done better than South America. Could it be because the Pilgrims came to American shores in search of God, whereas the people who came to South America were in search of gold?

182. The symbol of Christianity is the cross, not the feather bed.

183. Heinrich Heine was asked why men no longer built cathedrals like the one in Amiens. He said, "Then men had convictions, now they have opinions."

184. Massachusetts, Christmas, 1660 . . .
"Publik notice: The observation having been deemed a sacrilege, the exchanging of gifts and greetings, dressing in fine clothing, feasting and other satanical practices are hereby forbidden, with the offender liable to a fine of five shillings."

185. You're born   And then what?
     You go to school   And then what?
     You go to work   And then what?
     You retire   And then what?
     You die   And then what?

186. The world's scientists pooled all of their resources about the origins of the earth and humankind and fed all this into a giant linear program in the world's largest computer. Buttons were pressed. The computer groaned and moaned under the weight of this heavy stuff, lights blinked on and off, whistles tooted and bells rang. Then out came the printout:
"Read Genesis 1:1."

187. Every expert knows ways to curb juvenile delinquency. They all call for expenditures of huge sums of money. Spirituality is never mentioned.
     Crime would all but disappear if large doses of morality were applied.

188. There used to be three stagecoach fares:
First: If the stage gets stuck, sit still.
Second: If the stage gets stuck, get out.
Third: If the stage gets stuck, get out and push.
What sort of ticket does your spirituality have?

189. A little boy was lost. People looked desperately for days. Then all joined hands and went over the grounds again. They found the boy ... dead.
The boy's father said, "Oh, why didn't we join hands from the outset? Had we done that, my son would still be alive."

190. During a heat wave, a church put up this sign:
"And you think it's hot here."

191. Sign on church:
"Come in and have your faith lifted."

192. When that famous statue of Christ of the Andes was put in place, it faced Argentina. Christ's back was toward Chile. Chileans comforted themselves by saying, "Who needs watching more?"

193. Most unlikely church location: First Baptist Church at corner of Fifth and Bourbon.

194. "Son, what are you drawing a picture of?"
"God."
"But nobody knows what God looks like."
"They will after I get done with this picture."

195. "Tear God out of man's heart? Tell children that sin is only a fairy tale invented by their grandparents to make them behave. Print textbooks that ignore God and deride authority. Then don't be surprised what happens."
— Pope John Paul

196. All great thinkers filled with theorems and theories stand humbly, hat in hand, before a growing blade of grass.

197. If God seems too far away, which one of you moved?

198. When law has to be applied, religion has failed to do its job.

199. So you think you can get enough religion on radio and television. When you courted, did you call her up on the phone or did you go to see her?

200. To really enjoy stained-glass windows, you have to be inside the church.

201. If going to church makes you a Christian, then going to the garage makes you a car.

202. "I shall work as if everything depended on me and I'll pray as if everything depended on God."
— Saint Augustine

203. We're nuclear giants and spiritual infants.

204. Childhood prayer versions:
"Our Father, Howard be thy name."
"Lead us not into Penn Station."
"Our Father, who art in heaven, how'd you know my name?"

205. Religion ought to be a steering wheel, not a spare tire. ✓

206. Make us into living Bibles so those who cannot read the ⌢ Book can read the Book in us.

207. "Where was God when my son died in the Gulf War?" ⌒
"Exactly at the same place where he was when his son died on Calvary."

208. You may think you're moral when you're only uncomfortable.

209. Oh God, your sea is so big and my boat is so small.

210. Twice as many people attend church each Sunday as attend all sporting events for a year.

211. A man traveled from Jerusalem to Jericho and fell among thorns that sprung up and choked him. He finally got away and hitchhiked on a chariot that went under a sycamore tree. His hair got caught on a limb and he hung there for many days until the ravens came to feed him 500 loaves and two fish. Then Delilah came and cut his hair and he fell to the stony ground. When he got up it rained for forty days and forty nights so he hid in a cave and lived off locusts and wild honey. He was asked for dinner but he said he didn't want to come because he had married a wife, but the servants compelled him to come in and what a banquet it was ... twelve baskets of food remained. Blessed are the peacemakers. Now who's wife will she be on Judgment Day?

212. Baptists had trouble with people parking in their parking lot illegally. The problem was solved when they put up this sign: "No Parking. Violators will be baptized ... by immersion."

213. An Atlanta Baptist church had problems with Catholics parking in their parking lot. They cured this by putting this bumper sticker on Catholic cars: "I'm proud to be a Baptist."

214. The Spanish have a nice way of saying goodbye, "Vaya con Dios." Go with God!

215. A Pentecostal came to a Lutheran church. He had trouble wading through the liturgy. During the sermon, the pastor got warmed up and the Pentecostal shouted, "Praise the Lord."
Ushers grabbed the man. "You can't do that here."
"But I got the spirit."
"You didn't get it at this church."

216. Don't let the presence of hypocrites keep you out of church. There's always room for one more.

217. If you were arrested for being a Christian, would there be enough evidence to convict you?

218. To understand God's speed of light, think of it this way. If you shot a gun at the speed of light, the bullet would go around the world and hit you seven times before you could jump out of the way.

219. The Bible doesn't ask for money, it asks for people. If God has me, he has my money.

220. It's easier to learn to swim, ride a bicycle and learn a foreign language when you're young. It's the same thing with spirituality.

221. There were so many shotgun weddings performed in that church that they began calling it Winchester Cathedral.

222. Your poorest effort is more pleasing to God than your strongest excuses.

223. Sign on church: "God is alive and well . . . visiting hours twice on Sunday, at 8:30 and 11:00."

224. A new mission met in a barroom. The barroom parrot saw the minister and said, "New bartender." He saw the choir and said, "New floorshow." Then he looked at the people in the church and said, "Same old customers."

225. Dad taught me to believe in myself and Mom taught me to believe in God. I believe in both of them.

226. Preacher: "Everybody in this church is going to die." One man laughed: "I don't belong to this church."

√ 227. Church bulletin board: "Come early and get a back seat."

228. The church that doesn't pay attention to its youth need not worry about the future ... there won't be one.

229. Church is like a filling station. You can't run forever on one filling.

230. "God, I'm not asking you to move mountains. I can do that with bulldozers and dynamite. What I'm asking you to do is to move me."

231. "I was driven to my knees when there was no other place to go."   — Abraham Lincoln

√ √ 232. Tourist in Washington: "Do you expect the President to be in church this Sunday?"
      Pastor: "That I cannot promise, but we expect God to be here. We figure that should be incentive enough for a reasonably large attendance."

233. As late as 1933, churches administered ninety percent of the social agencies of the country. Then politicians thought they could improve on that, and the church allowed it to happen.

234. When wetlands legislation was placed on the books, bureaucracy reached new all-time records of aggravation. If there was a mud puddle on your property, you had to check first with the Corps of Engineers, then with the Fish and Wildlife Service, then with the Department of Natural Resources, then with the Soil Conservation Service, then with the Environmental Protection Agency before you could place a flower bed in that spot. That prompted the following story which gets a roar of laughter in rural areas where the bureaucracy has been painful.

God stood with Moses at the shore of the Red Sea. God said to Moses, "The good news is that I will part the waters so that the Children of Israel can go through. Then, when the Egyptians follow on the chase, I'll close the waters over the Egyptians and drown them."

Moses said, "What's the bad news?"

"First, you'll have to get permission from the Corps of Engineers, the Department of Natural Resources, the . . . (Every time I've told this story, laughter drowns out the rest of the line.)

235. In today's public schools, if a child is on his or her knees, that kid had better be playing craps and not praying.

236. Wouldn't it be something if, when you got to heaven, you found that your luggage went the other way?

237. Question asked in Sunday School: "Which virgin was Jesus' mother? The Virgin Mary or the King James Virgin?"

238. The Sunday School lesson dealt with Lot's wife.

"She looked back and was turned into a pillar of salt," the teacher said.

One fourth-grader commented, "My mother looked back once in our car and she turned into a telephone pole."

239. Cindy was a naughty girl. To punish her, her mother told her to sit in the corner. Cindy prayed, "I thank thee, Lord, for preparing a table before me in the presence of mine enemies."

240. New Ager: "There are no absolutes!"

"Are you sure?"

"Absolutely!"

Chapter 3

The People In The Pew

241. Thank God daily for the plurality of the Christian church in America. It is said about the people of the state churches of Europe: "He was in church three times in his life. Twice he had to be carried."

242. An atheist has no invisible means of support.

243. Preacher: "The tavern keeper makes all of the money. Who has the biggest car in town? The tavern keeper. Whose wife has the finest clothes? The tavern keeper's. Whose wife sits around the house all day, eating chocolates? The tavern keeper's. Who pays for all this? YOU DO."

A couple after the sermon: "Preacher, thank you for helping us to make up our minds."

Preacher: "Ah, so you are going to give up strong drink, are you?"

Couple: "No, we're going to buy a tavern."

244. "Father, I would consider it heaven if I could sit in the car in front of the house tooting the horn at seven a.m. while my husband got the kids dressed for mass."

245. Would you hire Goliath if you knew that David was looking for work?

246. Even network television anchors mispronounce names. Doctors of Divinity stumble through some of the unpronounceable names in the Bible. Lay people, teaching Bible Class, have the same problem.

Jim Evans taught his Bible Class a series from the book of Daniel. Reading from the text, he came upon these words, "At what time ye hear the sound of the cornet, flute, harp, sackbut, psaltery, dulcimer, and all kinds of music." He got through "flute" and "cornet" all right because he was familiar with those names, but he had never heard of a "sackbut" and "psaltery" floored him.

A few passages later, Jim stumbled through the passage again, as Daniel repeats it. His second time through wasn't a great improvement on the first reading. Then he encountered the list again. He looked. He shook his head. He looked up and said, "Folks, it's that same old band again."

247. Our Creator left poetry unwritten, songs unsung, inventions uninvented, continents undiscovered. In God's good time, he made it possible for man to write poetry, sing songs, to invent, and to discover.

248. When we're lost in a crowd, we seem to be insignificant, but to Christ, wherever we are, we are of immeasurable worth.

249. Both at midnight and at noon our clocks point their hands toward God. Do we acknowledge God's presence that often?

250. Cain and Abel told their parents that they found a most beautiful garden. "Why don't we move there?"

"We lived there once, but we ate ourselves out of house and home."

251. To impress the preacher who had dropped in for a visit, Mama told daughter, "Honey, bring me the good book that I read all of the time."

The daughter brought *TV Guide.*

252. Temporary atheist: Someone who hasn't won at Bingo for two months.

253. Preacher in pulpit: "Sister Smith, you don't need to take that cryin' baby out. He ain't botherin' me none."

"Maybe he ain't, Parson, but you sure are botherin' him."

254. The hymnal is the most ecumenical thing in Christendom. Catholics sing Martin Luther's "A Mighty Fortress Is Our God." Lutherans sing hymns written by Saint Gregory. Presbyterians sing Wesley's "Christ The Lord Is Risen Today." Baptists sing "Silent Night," written by a Roman Catholic choirmaster in the Austrian Tyrol.

255. "Who is this Dan and Beersheba?"

"They're not persons . . . they're towns."

"Oh, yeah. I always get them mixed up with the couple that the Bible calls Sodom and Gomorrah."

256. WHY I DO NOT GO TO THE MOVIES

1. The manager of the theater never called on me.
2. I went a few times, but nobody spoke to me. They're not friendly at the movies.
3. Every time I go to the movies, they ask for money.
4. Not all people at the movies live up to the high ethical standards of the movies.
5. I went so much as a kid ... I don't need the entertainment any more.
6. Lasts too long. I can't sit still for two hours.
7. I don't care for some of the people I see at the theater.
8. I don't always agree with what I see and hear at the movies.
9. The music isn't all that good at the picture show.
10. The shows are held in the evening, the only time I can be with my family.

257. After church:

"Do you think Madilyn Johnson is tinting her hair?"

"I don't know ... didn't see her."

"Do you think that dress that Mrs. Hansen was wearing should be paraded before the God-fearing people of the church?"

"I didn't notice that either."

"A lot of good it does you to go to church."

258. "Do you need proof of God?"

"Does one light a torch to see the sun?"

— Chinese maxim

259. Bible Class wisdom: "An epistle is the wife of an apostle."

56

260. Luther died by being excommunicated by a bull.

261. "Mr. Greeley, our church has tried everything . . . mock weddings, fairs, bazaars, plays, minstrel shows, rummage sales, donkey basketball, but we're still not getting there. What should we do?"
Horace Greeley: "Did you ever try Christ?"

262. A man was sleeping in church. The preacher figured out a way to wake him up. "Congregation, please rise for prayer. Brother Bob, will you lead?"
"Lead yourself, Reverend. I dealt last time."

263. "Father, what causes arthritis?"
"Fast living, drinking, carousing around, skipping mass. Why do you ask?"
"I see in the paper today that His Holiness has arthritis."

264. "What was the sermon about?"
"Don't worry . . . your quilts will come."
"You mean, 'Fear not, your comforter will come,' don't you?"

265. What's wrong with you kids? You can't understand these parables of Christ. Illiterate Galileans understood them.
They had a better teacher.

266. At the church meeting, the finances for the new organ were being discussed.
Modern Pharisee in the temple: "I'll match anything any one of the rest of you give."
Little old lady: "Mister, you and me has jist bought a new pipe organ for our church."

267. A kid came home all beat up.
"What happened to you?"
"I called the Pope a bad name."
"But didn't you know that the O'Rileys are Catholic?"
"Yeah, but I didn't know that the Pope was."

268. While the pastor called on the Stevensons, their youngest son came running into the house with a dead rat. His mother was aghast. "Don't worry, Mom. He's dead. Me and Jim, we bashed him until . . . (and then Junior noticed the pastor) . . . God called him home."

269. Our lives are made up of choices:
Judas chose thirty pieces of silver.
Peter chose denial.
Pilate acceded to the mob.
The high priests chose lies.
The people chose Barabbas.
Simon chose to carry the cross.

270. "Sister Smith, I think adultery is just as bad a sin as murder, don't you?"
"I doan know, Parson. I ain't never kilt nobody."

271. Sad commentary on the times: Overcrowded jails and undercrowded churches.

272. Puritans knew their Scripture so well that they would catch a single misquote in a two-hour sermon.

273. When he feels despondent he takes his rosary into a beautiful, wooded area. His wife's name is Rosary, by the way.

274. "Ah wants all da virgins in dis here congregation to stand," the preacher said.

Only one tall gal with a baby in her arms stood up.

"Sister Wilkins, I asked only da virgins to stand."

"Lawsy sakes, Parson, you don't spect dis little bitty baby can stand all by herself, do you?"

275. Oley stood at a second-story window during a Red River flood. A rowboat came along, but he turned it down. "The Lord will provide," Oley told the boatman. The water came higher, so Oley climbed through an attic window to the roof. There Oley turned down the offer of help from a helicopter. Again he said, "The Lord will provide." The Good Lord chose not to provide.

At the registration desk upstairs, Oley complained, "I thought you said you would provide."

"I provided you with a rowboat and a helicopter. When you turned both of them down, I figured you could swim."

276. Bill was going through Customs at O'Hare. The Customs Agent questioned a bottle in Bill's luggage.

Bill: "This is holy water from Guadalupe."

Agent: "It tastes like tequila."

Bill: "Praise the Lord; another miracle."

277. "Lord, don't let nothin' get hold of me today that you and me together cain't handle."

278. He knows the way of the Lord so well, he can find it in the dark.

279. Sunday School teacher: "What do we learn from Jonah and the whale?"
"People make whales sick to their stomachs."

280. Banker on the phone with a customer: "You say you want to convert your bonds. Don't you mean that you want to redeem them?"
Customer: "Who'm I talkin' to? The First Baptist Church or the First National Bank?"

281. As usual, Joe, in the last row of the balcony of the church, was asleep. This time the Rev. Smith decided to cure Joe once and for all. He began to wing it on the subject of hellfire and brimstone. He really made hell sizzle. When the pastor reached the pinnacle of terror, the pastor shouted: "Anybody in this church that wants to go to hell, STAND UP!"
Joe heard that "STAND UP" part of the sermon. He jumped to his feet.
Pastor: "Joe, do you know what you just voted for?"
"No, I don't, Preacher, but I see that you and me is the ones in favor of the proposition."

282. Lord, we thank you for the sense of smell ... onions in the stew, hickory smoke, spring lilacs, summer salt air, leaves burning in the fall, enchanting perfumes, chilled melons, fresh-cut limes, a newly-bathed infant, good wine, rain-soaked earth, hot bread, waxed wood, soft leather, jelly making, cake spice, oil paint, rubbed sage, candles on your altar.

Lord, we thank you for the sense of taste ... winter asparagus, spring lamb, summer strawberries, autumn pumpkin pies, birthday cakes, friendly toasts, hot coffee, crisp salad, fresh crackers, aged cheese, church suppers, ice cream, picnics, roast beef, family breakfasts, social luncheons, dinner out, midnight snacks.

Lord, we thank you for the sense of feel ... clean sheets, earned rest, morning dew, first frost, thawing breeze, good golf swings, saddle horses, tennis strokes, swimming power, full sails, relaxed muscles, hot baths, achievement, excitement, a child's kiss, a friendly embrace, ourselves expressed.

Lord, we thank you for the sense of hearing ... music, laughter, bird-song, family voices, spring rain, surf crash, dry leaves, squeaking snow, street sounds, friendly greetings, fireplace logs, good conversation, new ideas, machinery, jazz drums, summer insects, base hits, stadium cheers, card shuffles, popping corks, church bells, hymns, prayers.

283. "There are 10,000 stout fellows in London ready to fight to the death against popery, though they know not whether it be a man or a horse."   — Dr. Johnson

284. Country preacher: "In hellfire, there will be weepin' and wailin' and gnashin' of teeth."

"Parson, I ain't got no teeth."

"False teeth will be provided."

285. A Methodist minister inquired of a parishioner why he didn't come to church. He said it was because he had no good clothes and was ashamed to come to sit amongst those who were well-dressed. The preacher bought the man new clothes, but still, the next Sunday, he didn't come to church. After the 11:00 worship service, the charitable preacher went to visit the man. The man sat on the porch swing all dressed up in his fancy clothes.

"How come you didn't come to church today?"

"When I got all dressed up in these fancy duds, I looked so prosperous that I went to the Episcopal church."

286. "I am definitely opposed to buying a new chandelier for the church, for three reasons: (1) I can't spell chandelier. (2) If we got one, who's gonna play it? (3) If we got that kind of money in the treasury, why don't we buy a new light fixture for the church?"

287. A boy beat up an old lady; he knocked a kid off his bicycle; he threw rocks through a window. Said he was on the way to confession and had run out of material.

288. At the seminary, a professor gave the students some practice. He handed each a slip of paper and asked for comments. The first slip said, "Creation." The student replied, "In the beginning, God created the heaven and the earth." The next student received a card that said, "Justification." He quoted, "The just shall live by his faith." The next slip of paper said, "Constipation." This third student was equal to the assignment. He said, "And Moses took the two tablets and went into the wilderness."

289. "Johnny, do you know what we must do before our sins are forgiven?"

"We have to sin first."

290. Sol and Abe Ginsberg were invited to sit in on a service in the cathedral. They noted that the plate was passed three times and each time it came back full. After the mass, Sol asked if this was unusual. He was assured that it wasn't.

Sol turned to Abe and said, "How in the world did twelve Jews ever let this business slip out of their hands?"

291. Sunday School student: "A lie is an abomination unto the Lord, and a very present help in trouble."

292. In Sunday School: "The Jews have Thanksgiving too. They call it Passover. They eat unleavened bread. Does anyone here know what leaven is?"

"It comes just before twelve."

293. A wife told her drinking husband that if he didn't quit getting drunk all of the time, she would tell the priest and the priest would kick him out of the church. He stayed on the wagon for a while and then fell off. Drunk, he ran into his priest.

"Step aside, Father, and let a Protestant pass."

294. He dieted religiously . . . he quit snacking in church.

295. A farmer sold a visiting revival preacher a mule. He knew the critter was spavined and had the heaves, but he represented the critter to be "sound as a silver dollar."

Farmer's wife: "That was not nice."

Farmer: "I was following the biblical admonition that says, 'He was a stranger and I took him in.' "

296. A Lutheran boy took his friend, a Catholic boy, to church to see how things were done in the Lutheran church. He said, "When the pastor faces the altar, he is speaking to God for the whole congregation. When he faces the congregation, he speaks from God to the people." Then the pastor went into the pulpit and laid down his watch.

"What does that mean?" the Catholic boy wanted to know.

"Doesn't mean a doggoned thing."

297. Preacher: "Let anyone who considers himself perfect, stand up." One man stood up.

"You mean to say that you consider yourself perfect?"

"No, I don't. I'm a stand-in for my wife's first husband."

298. Two little kids, a boy and girl, fell into the water. They took off their clothes and hung them up to dry.

The little boy said, "I always wandered what the difference between a Presbyterian and a Catholic was."

299. Why I curse and swear:
1. To please my mother.
2. It's a fine mark of manliness.
3. It proves I have self-control.
4. It indicates how clearly my mind works.
5. It makes my conversation so pleasing.
6. It proves my good breeding.
7. It proves I have more than an ordinary education.
8. It makes me a desirable personality among men, women, and children . . . in all of respectable society.
9. It's my way of honoring God.

300. When a reporter from the *Times* checked at the heavenly registration desk, Saint Peter welcomed him profusely. He was given a suite that overlooked a beautiful lake with snow-capped mountains in the background. There was a butler and maid. Curiosity got the best of him. He asked Saint Peter why all of the ostentation. "Why me? I hear you have bishops in small rooms next to the furnace."

"Preachers, bishops, and even popes we got a lot of up here," Saint Peter said, "but you're the first newspaper man who has showed up in the last 87 years."

(Note: This twice-told tale doesn't have to have a newspaperman as the star of the show. It can be any other trade, business, or profession.)

301. Science can split atoms and build plastic cars, but it can't do much for a lay person's soul.

302. "So you say you don't go to church because the people there aren't perfect?"

"Yes."

"Glad to meet you, Mr. Kleen."

303. Before Great Smoky Mountains National Park was opened in 1935, most of the homes and farm buildings were removed. The churches and churchyards remain. In those churchyards there are many stones that memorialize the young ... many stones for children that lived only one day, one week, one year in days before antibiotics and penicillin. The messages that parents placed on these stones showed their spiritual devotion.

Epitaphs like: "Our little daughter is at rest in the mansion of the blest," and "Budded on earth to bloom in heaven."

304. Kathy knew she was driving recklessly. She rounded a curve, lost control, and totaled her car. When she came out of her coma in the hospital, she had an immediate relapse. She had glanced out of the window at the SHELL sign across the street. The lights behind the S were burned out.

305. The Steinberg brothers had the contract for painting the interior of the cathedral. While painting, they saw a ceremony rehearsal in the chancel that they were not familiar with. Father O'Riley explained that it was a rehearsal of the ceremony in which seven young women would become nuns. He said, "First the young women are novices, then novitiates; then they are married to Christ and given a wedding ring, and they become full-fledged nuns."

The Steinberg brothers asked if they could come and Father O'Riley said, "By all means."

When the Steinbergs came to the door of the nave, the ushers were puzzled. The brothers asked to be seated to the right. They explained, "Ve is relatives of da groom."

306. Sam agreed that if he married Sally, he would join her Catholic church. One day Sally's mother found her in tears. Her mother asked, "Why the crying?"

"Mother, I've oversold Sam on the Catholic Church. Now he wants to become a priest."

307. At this very moment, somewhere there is a woman who is trying to make up her mind whether she should order surgery on her only daughter — surgery that could claim her life. At this very moment, somewhere there is a man walking into a door marked MORGUE. His son didn't come home last night. At this very moment, there is a beautiful woman standing on a street corner, speaking with a man who is propositioning her. She's tempted. At this very moment, there is a man on a prison cot, contemplating tomorrow morning's gas chamber. At this very moment, I'm lying here comfortably, wondering if I should stay at home and catch up with my sleep tomorrow morning, or whether I should go to church to thank Almighty God for all of the blessings he has showered upon me.

308. A ventriloquist attended a funeral. As the casket was being lowered into the grave, a voice came from the bier, "Let me down easy, boys." "What happened then?" "I dunno. I didn't stay."

309. At prayer meeting, Mrs. Stevens had a long-winded prayer. Commenting about it, one of the parishioners said, "It was long, really long. That woman asked the Good Lord for things I didn't know he had."

310. As Charley drove through Homeville on a Sunday morning, he stopped to go to church. He sat down in a pew in back as the congregation intoned, "We have left undone those things we should have done, and we have done those things which we should not have done." Charley said to himself, "I have found my people."

311. Zelthy Harrison was the village hellion. For 83 years, she made life miserable for all around her. Then Zelthy died.
Her funeral was up in that little brown church on the rim. It was a hot, sultry day. All the mourners were fanning themselves with fans provided by Atchley Funeral Home. Then suddenly there was a bolt of lightning, followed immediately by a C-R-A-S-H of thunder. The little church on the rim trembled.
Dean Wilder was heard to say, "Zelthy got there. Thank you, Lord."

312. Three unchurched men were shipwrecked. They floated on a raft for three days without food and water. All of the ships they sighted did not see them. One of the men felt it was time to pray, but none of the three had ever been in a church.
Finally one said, "I grew up across the street from a Catholic church. Maybe I can help out. Bow your heads, fellows. Under I, 23. Under O, 44."

313. Across from St. Peter's Hospital stood St. Peter's High School. As a woman came out from under the anesthesia, she heard the high school band practicing for their next concert. She said to the nurse, "I hear music."
The nurse replied, "Yes, that's St. Peter's Band."
"Do you mean ...?"
"No, I don't mean."

314. A deaf-mute came to church each Sunday. He explained, "I know. I can't hear a thing, but I'm here to show the world which side I'm on."

315. You haven't been around the church long if you haven't gotten acquainted with people who are "agin" everything. Every denomination has them. Changes can't be made because "that isn't the way we've always done it." When you tell the following story, change the word "Lutheran" to any other suitable denomination.

"How many Lutherans does it take to change a light bulb?"

Answer: "Four. One to change the light bulb, and three to remind the congregation how much they liked the old light bulb."

316. That story prompts this one about a 100-year-old layman.

A reporter came from the paper to interview Grandpa Layman and get a picture. He said, "Grandpa, you've seen a lot of changes in your day, haven't you?"

"Yeah, Sonny, I have. An' I've been agin every durned one of them."

317. He prayed for a chicken and nothing happened. Then he prayed to the Lord to send him after a chicken. That got results.

318. The first 25 years of our lives we celebrate the body. The next 25, the mind. The last 25, we remember we have an immortal soul.

319. "Some people claim they are troubled by parts of the Bible that they do not understand. What troubles me is the parts of the Bible that I understand only too well."

— Mark Twain

320. A man stood on top of a building, threatening to jump. A crowd, including a policeman, gathered. The officer yelled, "Think of your parents." The man said he didn't have any. "Think of your wife and children, then." The man said he wasn't married. Then the Irish cop told the potential suicide victim, "Take out your beads and pray with me." The man said he didn't have a rosary.

The officer shouted, "Then jump, you lousy Protestant. You're tying up traffic."

321. A new cab driver, an Irishman, got a fare who asked to be taken to the Church of God. The cabbie took the man to St. Pat's cathedral.

"But that's not the Church of God."

"If God ain't in there, Buster, he ain't in town."

322. "I'm glad to see you in Sunday School, Jimmy."

"My dad said I couldn't go fishing with him."

"I hope he explained why."

"He said there weren't enough worms for the two of us."

323. Pat went to confession. He told the priest that he had committed adultery. The priest asked who with. Pat wouldn't answer.

"Was it the Widow Kelly, Katie O'Brien, or that young O'Leary girl?" Father Mulcahey asked. Pat assured the good Father that it was none of these.

Later in the day, Mike asked, "Pat, did you get absolution from the priest?"

"No, but I got three good prospects."

324. "Grandpa, how come you're reading the Bible so much lately?"
"I'm cramming for my finals."

325. A fighter in his corner crossed himself.
Fight fan in front row: "Do you think that will help him?"
The man beside him: "It will if he can fight."

326. The Friends Church burned, so the rabbi suggested they use the temple for their services. The two congregations got acquainted with each other. Two Jews joined the Friends Church.
The rabbi said, "Some of my best Jews are Friends."

327. An Orthodox Jew came to visit his son in a Georgia army camp. Both soldiers and civilians stared at him.
"Vot's da mot? You never seen a Yankee before?"

328. A drunk climbed into the bus and sat down next to a preacher, who was not amused.
"Mister, you are going straight to hell."
Drunk: "Hold it, driver. I'm on the wrong bus."

329. "I don't believe I'm going to marry Tom after all. He's an atheist. He doesn't believe in hell."
"Go ahead and marry him, Honey. Between the two of us, we should be able to convince him."

330. "Jed, you're an hour late getting back with the mules."
"I picked up the preacher on the way home and after he got on the wagon, them mules couldn't understand a word I said."

331. With Catholics, two words are important. "Rhythm" and "bingo." If you don't have rhythm, bingo!

332. Gallup poll:
1. Six out of ten teens can't name one of the four gospels.
2. Three out of ten don't know what happened on Easter.
3. Half can't recall five of the Ten Commandments.
4. A third don't know how many disciples there were.
Who flunked? The kids who didn't learn or the church that didn't teach? The nation is plagued with spiritual illiteracy and who's to blame?"

333. My uncle is why they invented locks.

334. At a dinner party attended by Mark Twain the subject of eternal life came up. Twain was silent. "Mr. Twain, what do you think?"
"I'm silent for good reason. I have friends in both places."

335. "Lord, give me patience, and give it to me RIGHT NOW!"

336. There's a shortage of birth control pills. Catholics have found that they're good for arthritis.

337. "What's that plaque behind the pulpit?"
"It's a tribute to the men who died in the service."
"The early service or the 10:30?"

338. "May you be in heaven a long time before the devil knows you're gone."   — Irish prayer

339. "Which of God's commandments is violated when you cut off a dog's tail?"
"What God hath joined together, let not man put asunder."

340. A Catholic woman complained, "They're changing so much in our church lately. Next thing you know, they'll substitute slot machines for bingo."

341. A topless woman walked into church.
An usher said, "Lady, you can't come in here that way."
"I have a divine right," she explained.
The usher replied, "The left isn't bad either, but you still can't come in."

342. An atheist is a person who goes to a Southern Methodist vs. Notre Dame game and doesn't give a rip who wins.

343. Her Protestant husband finally agreed to go to mass with her. On the way in, while gawking around, he upset the holy water. While staring at the frescos on the ceiling, he fell over his wife who was genuflecting. Then he stumbled over the kneeling bench. He sat down and wiped his brow, then held his handkerchief in his hand. His wife saw it and thought it was his shirttail.
She asked, "Is your zipper open?"
He replied, "No, should it be?"

344. Pat was known to steal lumber. The priest said he should make restitution.

"If you got the blueprints for a restitution, Father, I got the lumber."

345. Even Quakers can be crotchety. William abused the privilege. Then he died. Strain pervaded the funeral. All were silent. Then an elder said, "One thing thou canst say about William. At times he was not as bad as he was at other times."

346. A man asked a priest to bless his Ferrari. The priest said he didn't know what a Ferrari was. Ditto the Methodist minister. Then the man asked the Unitarian minister.

"I sure will. A Ferrari . . . 431 cubic inches . . . 0-60 in 5 seconds. By the way, what's a blessing?"

347. A Swede drove from Iron Mountain to Duluth. He had car trouble. He lifted the hood and began to pound. There were some choice words amongst the pounding.

Olaf's pastor saw the car stopped up ahead and recognized that it was Oley's car. He stopped to see if he could help. On the way to Oley's car, he heard all of those four-letter words.

"Oley, you're never going to get to heaven that way."

"Aye doan vant to get to heaven. Aye vant to get to Duluth."

348. There was an attempt to merge the Baptist with the Christian church.

A staunch Baptist exclaimed, "I was born a Baptist. I am a Baptist. I always will be a Baptist. They're not going to make a Christian out of me."

349. A Quaker's cow switched him in the face, stepped into the bucket, then kicked the bucket over.

He spoke to his cow: "Cow, thou knowest when thou aggravatest me with thy tail that I must hold my peace. Thou knowest that I could say naught when thou steppeth into the bucket, but what thou did not knowest was that when thou kicked the bucket over that I wouldst sell thee to a Methodist and I hope he kicks the hell out of you."

350. The goalie of the Red Wings took my son and me out to lunch. There we sat around the table: Father, Son, and Goalie host.

351. "How big is the Lutheran church?"

"Five and a half feet."

"What?"

Motioning with his hand at his neck, the boy explained, "My dad is six feet tall and he's said he's had it up to here with the Lutheran church."

352. He thought that high cholesterol was a religious holiday.

353. Catholics play bingo in Latin so Protestants can't win.

354. Quaker: "Take heed my friend. Thou mayest run thy face against my hand."

355. I got fired from the laundry because I went to the convent and asked the Mother Superior if the nuns had any dirty habits.

356. "We shouldn't be fishing on Sunday morning. We should be in church."

"I couldn't have gone anyway. My wife is sick and I would have had to stay home with her."

357. A Scotsman visited the Holy Land and asked the price of a boat rental on the Sea of Galilee. He was told, but retorted that he could rent a boat for half that sum in Aberdeen.

"But this is the sea on which the Good Lord walked."

"With your prices, it's nae wonder He walked."

358. Lincoln: I have been driven to my knees many times when I had an overwhelming conviction that there was no other place to go.

359. Baptists sin just like everybody else, but their religion forbids them to enjoy it.

360. "Aren't you afraid of flying?"

"Not a bit. If the plane goes down, I go up."

361. Artists in the Middle Ages concentrated their art on religious paintings. Michelangelo said, "The statue is already there in the marble. All I do is extract it."

362. I date back to the days when Christians were Christian and the plumbing was outdoors.

363. Deacon: A person who brings organized chaos out of regimented confusion.

364. If you run after money, you're materialistic. If you don't, you're a loser. If you get it and keep it, you're a miser. If you spend it, you're a spendthrift. If you don't work hard for it, you lack ambition. If you work hard for it, you are a fool who gets no fun out of life.

365. At the next church meeting, remember this: "You can't keep an open mind and open mouth at the same time."

366. A mustard seed and the seed of the General Sherman redwood are the same size — they both weigh 1/3,000th of an ounce. Do you remember that the Bible speaks of faith as small as a mustard seed?

367. In church work, remember that it is only 18 inches between a pat on the back and a kick in the pants.

368. Taking the line of least resistance tends to make men, roads, women, and rivers crooked.

369. One of every three people is ugly. In church, if the person to the left of you is not ugly and the person on the right of you is not ugly, I've got news for you.

370. "God cannot alter the past, but historians can."
— Samuel Butler

371. He's like a water faucet in a cheap hotel. Even when he's turned on, nothing happens.

372. Charley was the kind of guy who didn't have the sense that God gives a stump.

373. No matter how hard we try, we cannot completely comprehend God. For instance, what kind of secret ingredient does God put in concrete that makes grass grow in the cracks?

374. Eternity is like a barrel hoop — there's no end to it.

375. Believe it or not, in Wales, there's a church named Llanfairpwllgwyngyligogerychwyrndrobwillantysiliogogogoch." It means, "St. Mary's in a hollow of white hazel, near to a rapid whirlpool and also near St. Tysillio's Church, which is near a cave."

376. When Robert Emmet was being executed, peasants for miles around gathered to pray for the Irish patriot. One woman kneeled and was pushed aside. An English officer helped her to her feet and bawled out the soldier.

The peasant lady commented, "Thank you, Sir. If there's a cool spot in hell, I hope you get it."

377. Englishman: "Dreadfully sorry that you buried your wife at St. Basil's yesterday, Sir Sedgewick."

"Had to — she was dead, you know."

378. Pierre and Reggie came to America and became great friends. They walked to work together each day, and had a glass of beer afterward. One day Pierre hit Reggie.

"What was that for?"

"For you British killing our Saint Joan of Arc."

"But that was 500 years ago."

"That may be, but I only heard about it yesterday."

379. Chief Shortcake died of a heart attack along the road.

Chaplain to widow: "Do you want me to bury your husband?"

Widow: "No, squaw bury Shortcake."

380. "Why did the Pilgrims invite the Indians to Thanksgiving dinner?"

"Who else was there to invite?"

381. Pat strayed through the cemetery drunk one night. He fell into an open grave. He awoke in the morning as the sun caught his eyes.

"Praise tha Lord. 'Tis Judgment Day, so it is, and I'm the first one up."

382. Pat was going back to his birthplace, Belfast, after many years away. He asked a friend, "What do I do about this Catholic/Protestant thing?"

His friend explained, "If you're in the Catholic end of town, you're Catholic. If you're in the Protestant end of town, you're Protestant. It's as simple as that."

When the train arrived at 9:30 p.m. Pat couldn't wait. He took a quick walk around several blocks near the station. On a dark street a man jumped out of an alley and held a gun at Pat's head. He didn't know which end of town he was in.

Robber: "Catholic or Protestant?"

Pat said, "Jew."

Robber: "I've got to be the luckiest Arab in Ireland."

383. A Jew was sent to the pest house. He was asked if he wanted religious consolation. He answered, "Yes, send me Father O'Brien."

"Are you sure? Wouldn't you prefer a rabbi?"

"Do you tink I vant to gif Rabbi Steinberg the small pox?"

384. They've got Affirmative Action in Israel too. The government insisted that the Sanhedrin had to be ten percent Samaritan.

385. Adam and Eve were the first Communists. They had no clothes, no home, little to eat, and yet they believed they were in paradise.

386. "How many potatoes are there in Russia?"

"If placed all together, they would reach the feet of God."

"But we Communists believe that there is no God."

"There are no potatoes, either."

387. Chelenko had just arrived in heaven. He told Saint Peter . . .

"There is religious freedom in Russia. I proclaimed the glory of God the Father, Son, and Holy Spirit right in the middle of Red Square."

"When did that happen?"

"About three minutes ago."

388. Olga: "I hate you, Swen. We've been married 43 years and we have fought all 43. I don't want any more of it. I don't want a divorce. Let's pray the Good Lord to take one of us home. Then I can go and live with my sister in Kansas."

389. Oley prayed: "Good Lord, I got a notice from the Federal Land Bank that they are about ready to take over the farm if I don't pay up. I haven't got the money. Good Lord, you're Norwegian and I'm Norwegian. Help me to save the farm that has been in the Torgelson family for three generations. Good Lord, help me to win the lottery." He didn't win.

The next Sunday, Oley prayed again: "Good Lord, didn't you hear me? This is your obedient servant, Olaf Torgelson. I've got to win the lottery to save the farm that has been in our family for three generations. Please, Lord, help me to win the lottery." He didn't win. The Federal Land Bank repossessed the Torgelson farm.

In tears, Oley prayed again: "Good Lord, why did you let me down? I'm Norwegian and you're Norwegian. Now the farm is gone. What am I gonna do? Oh, why did you fail me, Lord?"

A voice came from the clouds: "Olaf, you could have met me halfway. You could have bought a lottery ticket."

390. Scottie lay dying. The Presbyterian pastor and the family were gathered around the death bed. There was silence except for an occasional sob and the pastor's prayers. Then Scottie motioned with his finger for the pastor to come to the side of the bed. Scottie placed a gold watch into the pastor's hands.

"Reverend, how would you like to buy a good watch?"

391. A Scotsman gave his wife an X-ray picture of his chest. He wanted her to know that his heart was in the right place.

392. Scottie broke off his engagement when he found a girl in Aberdeen whose birthday is on Christmas.

393. Near a Presbyterian church in Scotland, there was a rickety bridge that had a KEEP OFF sign. An American tourist ventured out on it anyway. One of the locals said, "Stop."

The tourist explained, "We're tourists from America and we're Presbyterian. I just wanted to take a picture of this church from another angle."

The local explained about the rickety bridge. "A dinna care aboot that, Laddie, but if you go much further, you're gonna become a Baptist."

Chapter 4

Stewardship

394. At church we often hear, "O don't tell me. They want money again? What's it for this time? You know how bad business has been lately."

At the country club, we hear things differently:

"Why, for only $3,600 initiation fees and $2,500 for a full year's dues, you get golf, swimming, tennis, a health spa, dining and bar privileges. A real bargain!"

395. Of a steward nothing more is required than that the steward be found faithful. And nothing less.

396. The sermon went longer than usual.

"Mommy, if we pay our money now, will he let us go?"

397. Preacher: "Get all you can."

"Amen."

"Give all you can."

"Preacher, why you mess up a good sermon, huh?"

398. If everyone on welfare tithed, and no one else gave a cent to church, we would have 35 percent more contributions than we have now.

399. Using man's arithmetic, when you subtract, you have less. Using God's arithmetic, when you give something to him, you have more left than what you started with.

400. Dr. Harris, a Methodist preacher, told a columnist that people who did not support the church were parasites. The columnist used the quote in a column. Dr. Harris got 600 nasty letters.

Harris commented, "I didn't know that parasites were sensitive."

401. "Whoops, I dropped a $20 into the plate instead of a one. Can I have it back?"

"No, the Lord gives no refunds."

"Then I have $20 credit with the Lord."

"No, only $1. That's what you intended to give. For the Lord, the other nineteen bucks are gravy."

402. "We want to thank Widow Jones for the unusually large gift she gave the church last Sunday. Today we give her the privilege of picking three hymns."

Pointing to men, she said, "I'll take him, and him, and him."

403. You can't take it with you, but you can send it on ahead.

404. Plaque in the C. Y. Stephens Auditorium at Iowa State:

"I would have liked to have written a fine poem or a great book, or possibly made a worthy discovery in science, but since all these accomplishments have been denied me, I shall use my ability to accumulate money in such a manner that will make it possible for many others to do the things I would have done."

405. At the carnival the strong man squeezed an orange. Then he offered $5 to anyone who could squeeze another drop out of it. A man came forward and got five drops.

"I've never seen that happen before. What do you do?"

"I'm treasurer at St. Paul's Lutheran Church."

406. "Our preacher man done absconded with the funds. We caught up with the varmint up by Humeville. He had the money all spent. Spent part of the money on women and the rest he spent foolishly. We got him now and we're bringin' him back and we're gonna make him preach what he owes us."

407. One of the best tests of a religion is to find yourself in church with nothing but a $20 bill.

408. The parishioners of this church in Iowa used to put IOUs in the plate. The parishioners paid at the end of the month on the basis of what they thought the sermons were worth.
One month one man wrote, "You owe me ten bucks."

409. "This business of Christianity is just one constant give, give, give."
Pastor: "Thank you. That's the finest definition of Christianity I've heard in a month of Sundays."

Index

Your author realizes that a reference book is as good as its index. When you want to find something, you want to find it! Perhaps you remember one word of a story, but don't recall the punch line. This index is *complete!* If you know that one word, you'll find it in the index, or the story is not in this book.

antagonize 140
apologize 149
apostles 177, 259
approbation 157
appropriate 46, 144
Argentina 192
arithmetic 399
ark 24
armed services 30
Armstrong, Louis 77
army 145
army camp 327
arrested 217
arrive 387
arrow 90
arthritis 263, 336
artist 361
ashamed 285
ask 59, 69, 129, 138, 169, 219,
  256, 309
  (for directions) 138
  (for money) 256
asleep 130, 158, 281
atheist 242, 252, 329, 342
attempt 348
attend church 164, 210
attendance 232
attendant 6
attic 275
auditorium 404
Augustine, Saint 202
Austria 254
author 147, 153
automatic 20
automobile 14, 116, 121, 201,
  244, 301
awake 174
awful 150

B
baby 13, 253, 274
back 121, 161, 227
  (room) 161
  (seat) 121, 227

bad name 267
bad news 234
baggage 148
bait 105
balcony 47, 281
ball game 99, 155
band 47, 246, 313
  (practice) 313
bank, banker 280
banquet 19, 70, 75
Baptist 39, 53, 82, 123, 124,
  144, 158, 212
  (minister) 144
Baptist Church 174, 193, 213
baptize 212
bar 32, 65, 85, 224, 394
  (privileges) 394
  (room) 85, 224
  (tender) 224
Barabbas 270
barbed wire fence 74
bargain 394
barn 116
Barnabas, Saint 90
barrel hoop 374
bartender 32
Bartholdi, Fred 171
Bartholomew, Saint 90
basement 20
batter up 99
battlefield 9
Bayer aspirin 170
bazaar 261
be careful 23
beach 174
beads (also see rosary) 132
beard 61
beat up 267
beautiful young woman 43, 79,
  105, 307
bed 88
beer 3, 378
behave 195
beheaded 90

Dan and Beersheba 255
dancing 102, 158
Daniel 246
dark, darkness 178, 278
date back 362
daughter 251, 307
davenport 67
David 245
day off 155
deacon 91, 117, 363
dead, death 111, 189, 268, 377,
    390
    (bed) 390
    (mule) 111
    (rat) 268
deaf-mute 314
deal 262
deceiver 150
deciding vote 171
Declaration of Independence 171
definition 409
delay 27
democracy 177
demur 157
deny, denial 269, 404
Department of Natural
    Resources 234
depend 202
deride 195
desirable 299
despair 178
desperate 189
despondent 273
destroy 50
devil 338
Dial soap 170
die 65, 178, 185, 226, 260, 311,
    345, 388, 390
diet 79, 294
differ 57
difference 109, 298
dining room 394
dinner 80, 334, 380
    (party) 334

dirty habits 355
disappear 187
disciples 332
discord 178
discount 1
discover 404
discuss 266
disrespectful 125
dissent 143
distress 115
divine right 341
divorce 388
doctor 40, 48, 118, 246
    (of divinity) 40, 246
    ('s office) 48
doctorate 40
doctrine 57
doesn't mean a thing 296
dog 24, 339
dollar 10
donkey basketball 261
door 69, 82
    (prize) 82
doorbell 69
dose 187
doubt 178
downtown church 154
drag 90
drawing a picture 194
dress 8, 125, 244, 257
drill field 145
drink 29, 32, 39, 55, 158, 263,
    293
drive 124, 304, 310
    (through) 310
driver 328
drop 166
drought 123
drunk 59, 63, 99, 328
DT's 65
dues 394
dulcimer 246
dynamite 230

Goliath 245
good 22, 34, 91, 103, 107, 132, 234
  (crop) 22
  (deed) 91
  (looking) 34
  (manners) 132
  (news) 234
  (people) 103
goodbye 214
Gospel 332
gossip 39
got out of the way 149
governor 171
grandparents 195, 316, 324
grass 373
grasshopper 91
Great Smoky Mountains National Park 303
Greece 90
Greeley, Horace 261
green 49
greetings 184
Gregory, Saint 254
gripe 88
grocery cart 3
groom 119, 305
group counseling 27
grow 196, 373
Guadalupe 276
guess 31
guest 145
guide 174
Gulf War 207
gun 16, 63, 218
gutter 44

H
haberdashery 60
habits 355
had 106, 351
  (enough) 106
  (it up to here) 351

hail 91
hair 211
Hallmark 170
ham 82
hand 127, 249, 354
  (out) 127
handkerchief 343
handle 277
hang 90, 100
  (-ed himself) 100
happen 267
hard hat 174
Harlem 77
harp 246
hat in hand 196
hatred 178
have that honor 19
head 148
Health Department 111
health spa 394
hear 1, 62, 394, 409
  (confessions) 62
heard 378
heart 195, 391
  (in the right place) 391
heat wave 190
heating oil 97
heaven 98, 128, 158, 161, 204, 236, 244, 338, 387
heaves 295
Heine, Heinrich 183
helicopter 275
hell 34, 98, 281, 284, 328, 329, 376
  (-fire) 284
hellion 311
help yourself 95
heresy 50
Heropolis 90
Hezekiah 104
hiccups 48
hide 69
hierarchy 31

W

wagon 330
wailing 284
wait until the last minute 6
waiter 144
waitress 75
wake up 262
Wales 375
walk, walked 105, 357, 378
warmed up 215
Washington, D.C. 232
Washington, George 71, 171
watch 192, 296, 390
water faucet 371
watermelon 94, 144
weaned 122
wedding 72, 120, 261
   (car) 72
weeping 284
welfare 398
well 67
Wesley, Samuel 254
wetlands legislation 234
whale 279
wheel 114
whiskey 121, 124
whisper 8, 34
white 61, 179
   (church) 179
   (robe) 61
wide 157
widow 83, 379, 402
wife 8, 24, 28, 49, 54, 65, 113,
   151, 243, 259, 293, 297, 356
wild animal 16, 51
wild women 55, 406
wilderness 168, 288
win 35
Winchester Cathedral 221
window 275, 287
wipe 343
wise, wisdom 15, 259
with you in spirit 145

wizard 131
woman 25, 34, 39, 43, 60, 74,
   89, 149, 266, 274, 307, 340,
   341, 368, 376
wonder 307
Wonder Bread 135
wondered 156
word 46
work 170, 185, 202, 245
   (wonders) 170
worms 322
worry 228
worship 174, 180
wreck 304
write 49, 56, 404
   (a book) 49
writer 141
wrong 85, 165, 265, 328
   (bus) 328
   (idea) 165
   (number) 85

X

X-ray 391

Y

Yankee 99, 327
   (Stadium) 99
year 88
yell 12
young 43, 59, 106, 303
   (woman) 43, 59
youth 228

Z

zipper 343